The Transformer Architecture

A Practical Guide to Natural Language Processing

Tommy Hogan

Copyright © 2023 by Tommy Hogan

Table of Contents

Introduction

1. Understanding Natural Language Processing

Natural Language Processing (NLP) is the remarkable field where machines learn to comprehend, decipher, and even generate human language. Think of it as the bridge between how we communicate naturally and how computers analyze data. This bridge opens up a world of possibilities, from chatbots that talk to us like humans to translating languages in real-time and gauging sentiment in text.

NLP has come a long way, and this book will be your guide to understanding one of its game-changing advancements: the Transformer architecture.

In essence, NLP empowers computers to work with human language in meaningful ways. It enables them to read text, understand its context, and respond intelligently. This has revolutionized countless industries, from customer service and content recommendation to healthcare and finance.

Imagine a world where computers can read and summarize documents, translate languages on the fly, answer questions, and even generate creative content like poetry or stories. NLP brings us closer to that reality, and the Transformer architecture is a pivotal part of this journey.

2. The Rise of Transformers

The Transformer architecture is the rising star of NLP. It burst onto the scene in 2017 through a groundbreaking research paper titled "Attention is All You Need" by Vaswani and his colleagues. Since then, Transformers have become the backbone of state-of-the-art NLP models.

At the heart of the Transformers' success is its self-attention mechanism. This innovative technique allows models to focus on different parts of input text with varying levels of attention. It's like giving the model the ability to pay more attention to the important words and less to the irrelevant ones, just as a human would. This context-awareness has elevated Transformers above other approaches, enabling them to understand language nuances, context, and relationships effectively.

Transformers have revolutionized the way we approach NLP tasks. They excel in a wide range of language-related tasks, from machine translation and document summarization to sentiment analysis and question-answering systems. Their adaptability and performance have made them indispensable in today's NLP landscape.

3. Goals and Scope of This Book

Our primary aim with this book is to provide you with a practical grasp of the Transformer architecture and how to apply it in NLP. We'll take you on a journey, starting with the fundamental concepts and gradually leading you towards hands-on implementation. By the end of this book, you'll have the knowledge and skills to build and fine-tune your own Transformer models for various NLP tasks.

This book is designed to be your companion on your NLP and Transformer adventure. Whether you're a novice looking to understand the basics or an experienced practitioner aiming to master Transformers, we've got you covered. We believe in learning by doing, so you can expect practical examples and exercises to reinforce your understanding.

4. Prerequisites and Assumptions

To make the most of this book, a basic understanding of machine learning concepts will be helpful. Familiarity with Python programming is essential since we'll be using it extensively. While prior experience with popular machine learning libraries like TensorFlow and PyTorch is beneficial, it's not mandatory. We'll provide code samples and explanations throughout the book to ensure that you can follow along even if you're new to these libraries.

Our goal is to make this book accessible and engaging for learners of all levels. So, whether you're just starting your journey in NLP or looking to take your skills to the next level with Transformers, we're excited to have you on board.

Now, let's get started with the exciting journey into the world of Transformers and Natural Language Processing!

Dear Readers,

Your thoughts matter to us! If this book brought a smile or a moment of respite at the end, please consider sharing your experience through a review. Your feedback is invaluable in making our books even more enjoyable for fellow NLP and AI enthusiasts.

Thank you for your support!

Chapter 1: Fundamentals of Transformers

In this chapter, we will lay the foundation for understanding Transformers, one of the most influential innovations in the field of Natural Language Processing (NLP). We will explore how Transformers came into existence, dissect their key components, and provide an overview of the Transformer architecture.

1.1. The Birth of Transformers

The story of Transformers, the revolutionary architecture in Natural Language Processing (NLP), begins with a landmark paper titled "Attention is All You Need," authored by Vaswani et al. in 2017. This paper is akin to the birth certificate of Transformers, and it introduced a fundamentally new way of processing language data that has since reshaped the NLP landscape.

Before Transformers, traditional NLP models primarily relied on recurrent neural networks (RNNs) and convolutional neural networks (CNNs) to handle sequences of data, such as sentences or paragraphs. While these models were effective to some extent, they had limitations, especially when it came to capturing long-range dependencies within the text.

The groundbreaking idea that Transformers brought to the forefront was the concept of the self-attention mechanism. Here's what makes it so remarkable:

Self-Attention Mechanism: Transformers employ a mechanism that allows them to weigh the importance of different words or tokens in a sequence when processing it. Imagine reading a long article; you naturally pay more attention to certain words or phrases that seem crucial for understanding the content. This is similar to what the self-attention mechanism does, but at an incredible scale.

This self-attention mechanism became the secret sauce of Transformers. It enables these models to process each word in a sentence while considering all other words, assigning varying degrees of attention based on context. This ability to capture context across the entire sequence, rather than just looking at adjacent words (as in RNNs), was a game-changer. It allows Transformers to understand language nuances, relationships, and dependencies that were previously challenging for other models.

With the self-attention mechanism as its core, the Transformer architecture showed its prowess in various NLP tasks. It excelled in machine translation, text summarization, question-answering, sentiment analysis, and more. The key strength lay in its adaptability and context-awareness. It could handle both short and long sentences, grasp intricate grammatical structures, and adapt to different languages seamlessly.

The introduction of Transformers represented a turning point in NLP research and application. It shifted the focus from designing task-specific models to creating a single architecture that could be fine-tuned for various tasks—a paradigm shift that led to greater efficiency and remarkable performance gains.

In summary, the birth of Transformers was marked by the introduction of the self-attention mechanism in the "Attention is All You Need" paper. This mechanism's ability to capture context across sequences with remarkable efficiency paved the way for a new era in NLP, where understanding the intricacies of human language became more accessible and powerful than ever before. This chapter sets the stage for us to explore the key components and capabilities of Transformers in more detail.

1.2. Key Components of Transformers

Transformers, the trailblazing architecture behind modern Natural Language Processing (NLP) breakthroughs, consist of several key components. Understanding these components is pivotal to comprehending how Transformers work and why they are so effective in handling language tasks. Let's get into each of these components in detail:

1. Self-Attention Mechanism:

At the core of the Transformer lies the self-attention mechanism. This mechanism is what grants Transformers their remarkable ability to process sequences of data, such as words in a sentence, by assigning varying degrees of attention to different elements based on their context.

Imagine you're reading a book, and you come across a pronoun like "it." To understand "it," you naturally look back in the text to find what "it" refers to. This is akin to what the self-attention mechanism does for each word in a sentence. It assesses the relevance of every word in relation to the word being processed, allowing the model to understand the context effectively.

.2. Positional Encoding:

Unlike recurrent neural networks (RNNs) that inherently understand word order due to their sequential nature, Transformers treat input data as sets without inherent positional information. To address this, Transformers use positional encoding.

Positional encoding is a set of vectors added to the input embeddings to convey information about the position of each word in a sequence. This encoding ensures that the model recognizes the order of words in a sentence, enabling it to understand the text's structure.

3. Multi-Head Attention:

Transformers take self-attention a step further with multi-head attention. Instead of relying on a single attention mechanism, they employ multiple heads, each responsible for attending to different aspects of the input.

This multi-head approach enables Transformers to capture different types of relationships and dependencies within the text. It's like having multiple experts in the room, each focusing on specific aspects of the problem, and then combining their insights to make a more informed decision.

4. Feedforward Neural Networks:

In addition to self-attention, Transformers employ feedforward neural networks. These networks are responsible for further processing the information gathered through self-attention.

The output from the self-attention mechanism is rich in context but may require additional refinement. Feedforward networks, through a series of linear transformations and activation functions, enhance the model's ability to learn complex patterns and representations from the input data.

5. Layer Normalization:

Layer normalization is a technique used within Transformers to stabilize training and improve their performance. It operates at each layer of the model, ensuring that the input to each layer has a consistent distribution.

This normalization helps mitigate issues like vanishing gradients during training, making it easier to train deep Transformer models effectively. As a result, Transformers can capture intricate linguistic nuances in longer sequences without encountering instability.

Understanding these key components sets the stage for grasping how Transformers process and analyze language data. Each component plays a crucial role in the model's ability to understand context, relationships, and dependencies, making Transformers the powerhouse they are in modern NLP. In the upcoming chapters, we'll explore how these components work together to perform tasks like machine translation, text summarization, and sentiment analysis.

1.3. Transformer Architecture Overview

The Transformer architecture represents a pivotal shift in Natural Language Processing (NLP). To appreciate its significance, let's reach into an overview of this revolutionary structure, which is the driving force behind many state-of-the-art NLP models:

Encoder-Decoder Structure:

Transformers typically follow an encoder-decoder structure, particularly when tackling sequence-to-sequence tasks like machine translation. This structure consists of two main components: the encoder and the decoder.

1. Encoder: The encoder is responsible for processing the input sequence, be it a sentence in one language for translation or any other sequence-based input. It breaks down the input into a format that can be effectively understood by the model.

2. Decoder: The decoder takes the information encoded by the encoder and generates the output sequence, such as the translation in the target language. It's essentially responsible for producing the desired result based on the input and learned representations.

Stacked Layers:

Both the encoder and decoder in Transformers consist of multiple layers, typically stacked on top of each other. Each layer is identical in structure, allowing for a deep architecture. The depth is one of the factors contributing to the Transformer's ability to capture complex patterns and relationships in data.

Self-Attention Mechanism:

At the heart of each layer in the Transformer is the self-attention mechanism. This mechanism is a pivotal innovation that enables the model to understand the context and relationships between words in a sequence.

Self-attention works by assigning varying degrees of attention to different words in the input sequence. It allows the model to weigh the importance of each word based on the context, capturing long-range dependencies and relationships effectively. This context-awareness is what makes Transformers excel in NLP tasks.

Positional Encoding:

Since Transformers treat input data as sets rather than sequences, they need a way to incorporate positional information. Positional encoding is a technique used to embed this positional information into the input embeddings. It ensures that the model understands the order of words in a sentence or the position of elements in the input set.

Multi-Head Attention:

Transformers take self-attention a step further with multi-head attention. Instead of relying on a single attention mechanism, they employ multiple heads, each responsible for learning different aspects of the data.

Multi-head attention enables Transformers to capture various relationships and dependencies simultaneously. It's like having multiple experts analyzing different facets of the input, which collectively leads to a more comprehensive understanding.

Feedforward Neural Networks:

Within each layer of the Transformer, there are feedforward neural networks. These networks further process the information obtained through self-attention and multi-head attention.

The feedforward networks consist of linear transformations followed by activation functions, allowing the model to learn complex patterns and representations from the input data.

Layer Normalization:

Layer normalization is applied at various points within the Transformer architecture. It ensures that the input to each layer has a consistent distribution, which stabilizes training and makes it easier to train deep Transformer models effectively.

By incorporating all these elements, Transformers have revolutionized NLP. They can handle sequences of varying lengths, capture intricate language structures, and adapt to multiple languages and tasks. Whether it's translating languages, summarizing text, or understanding sentiment, the Transformer architecture's versatility and context-awareness have made it an indispensable tool in modern NLP.

This overview sets the stage for our deeper exploration of Transformers in subsequent chapters, where we'll get into their application in various NLP tasks and provide hands-on examples to illustrate their capabilities.

Chapter 2: Preprocessing and Data Preparation

In this chapter, we embark on the journey of transforming raw text data into a format suitable for training Transformer models. Effective preprocessing and data preparation are essential steps to ensure that the data is well-structured, informative, and ready for machine learning. We will explore the following key aspects in detail:

2.1. Data Collection and Cleaning

Data collection and cleaning are foundational steps in any Natural Language Processing (NLP) project. In this section, we'll explore the intricacies of gathering data and preparing it for analysis with Transformers. We'll also provide code examples to illustrate the concepts.

Data Collection:

1. Web Scraping: When collecting text data from the internet, web scraping is a common approach. Python libraries like BeautifulSoup and requests make it easy to fetch web pages and extract text.

```python
import requests
from bs4 import BeautifulSoup

# Fetch a webpage
url = 'https://example.com'
response = requests.get(url)

# Parse HTML content
soup = BeautifulSoup(response.text, 'html.parser')

# Extract text
text = soup.get_text()
```

2. Accessing Existing Datasets: Many NLP tasks can benefit from publicly available datasets. Libraries like `nltk` or `datasets` provide convenient ways to access and load these datasets.

```python
import nltk
nltk.download('movie_reviews')
from nltk.corpus import movie_reviews

# Access the movie_reviews dataset
documents = [(list(movie_reviews.words(fileid)),
category)
        for category in movie_reviews.categories()
        for fileid in movie_reviews.fileids(category)]
```

Data Cleaning:

3. Removing Duplicates: Duplicate records can skew your analysis. You can identify and remove duplicates based on content or specific columns.

```python
import pandas as pd

# Load a dataset
data = pd.read_csv('your_dataset.csv')

# Remove duplicates based on a specific column
data = data.drop_duplicates(subset='text_column')
```

4. *Handling Missing Values*: Missing data can be problematic. You can either remove rows with missing values or impute missing values using techniques like mean imputation.

```
# Remove rows with missing values
data = data.dropna()
```

```
# Impute missing values with the mean
data['numerical_column'].fillna(data['numerical_colu
mn'].mean(), inplace=True)
```

5. Text Cleaning: Text data often contains noise like HTML tags, special characters, and punctuation. Regular expressions can help clean text.

```
import re
```

```
# Remove HTML tags
text = re.sub('<.*?>', '', text)
```

```
# Remove special characters and punctuation
```

```
text = re.sub('[^A-Za-z0-9]+', ' ', text)
```

6. Lowercasing: Consistently converting text to lowercase can help with uniformity in your dataset.

```
# Convert text to lowercase
text = text.lower()
```

These data collection and cleaning techniques are crucial for preparing your text data for further analysis with Transformers. Whether you're gathering data from the web, using existing datasets, or cleaning text, attention to detail in this phase greatly influences the quality of your NLP project.

2.2. Tokenization and Vocabulary

Tokenization and vocabulary building are pivotal steps in preprocessing text data for Transformers. They enable the model to understand and work with textual information. Let's explore these concepts in detail:

Tokenization:

1. What is Tokenization?: Tokenization is the process of breaking down text into smaller units, called tokens. Tokens can be words, subwords, or characters, depending on the chosen tokenization method.

2. Word Tokenization: In word tokenization, text is split into individual words. This is a common approach when working with English text.

```python
import nltk
nltk.download('punkt')
from nltk.tokenize import word_tokenize

text = "Tokenization is important for NLP."
tokens = word_tokenize(text)
print(tokens)
```

Output:

```
['Tokenization', 'is', 'important', 'for', 'NLP', '.']
```

3. Subword Tokenization: Subword tokenization, such as Byte Pair Encoding (BPE) or SentencePiece, divides text into smaller units that might not always correspond to complete words. This is particularly useful for handling languages with complex word formation.

```
# Using the Hugging Face Transformers library
from transformers import BertTokenizer

tokenizer = BertTokenizer.from_pretrained('bert-base-uncased')
text = "Tokenization is important for NLP."
tokens = tokenizer.tokenize(text)
print(tokens)
```

Output:
['token', '##ization', 'is', 'important', 'for', 'nl', '##p', '.']

Vocabulary Building:

4. What is a Vocabulary?: A vocabulary is a collection of unique tokens used in a specific NLP task. It maps tokens to numerical IDs, allowing the model to work with text as numerical data.

5. Building a Vocabulary: You can build a vocabulary from your tokenized data. It's essential to consider the vocabulary size, which impacts the model's memory usage and training speed.

```
# Using the Hugging Face Transformers library
from transformers import BertTokenizer

tokenizer                                        =
BertTokenizer.from_pretrained('bert-base-uncased')
text = "Tokenization is important for NLP."
tokens = tokenizer.tokenize(text)

# Build a vocabulary
vocab = tokenizer.get_vocab()
print(vocab)
```

Output:

{'[PAD]': 0, '[CLS]': 1, '[SEP]': 2, '[MASK]': 3, 'token': 4, '##ization': 5, 'is': 6, 'important': 7, 'for': 8, 'nl': 9, '##p': 10, '.': 11}

6. Mapping Tokens to IDs: Once you have a vocabulary, you can map tokens to numerical IDs.

```
# Map tokens to IDs
token_ids = [vocab[token] for token in tokens]
print(token_ids)
```

Output:

[4, 5, 6, 7, 8, 9, 10, 11]

Tokenization and vocabulary building are essential for preparing text data for Transformer models. They enable the model to understand and process text, setting the stage for effective training and analysis. Proper choices in tokenization and vocabulary size can significantly impact model performance and efficiency in handling text data.

2.3. Data Encoding and Padding

Data encoding and padding are critical steps in preparing text data for training Transformer models. These processes enable the model to work with text efficiently and ensure uniform input dimensions. Let's deal with these concepts in detail:

Data Encoding:

1. Numerical Representation: Transformer models require text data to be converted into a numerical format. This is typically achieved by mapping tokens to numerical IDs using a vocabulary.

2. One-Hot Encoding: In traditional NLP, one-hot encoding is used, where each token is represented as a binary vector with a length equal to the vocabulary size. Only the position corresponding to the token's ID is set to 1, while others are 0. However, this approach results in high memory consumption for large vocabularies and lacks contextual information.

3. Word Embeddings: A more efficient approach is to use word embeddings, which represent tokens as dense, continuous-valued vectors. Word2Vec, GloVe, and pre-trained transformer-based embeddings (e.g., Word2Vec) are commonly used. These embeddings capture semantic relationships between words and allow the model to understand the context.

```
# Using pre-trained word embeddings (e.g., Word2Vec)
import gensim.downloader as api

# Load pre-trained embeddings
word_vectors                                    =
api.load("word2vec-google-news-300")

# Encode tokens using embeddings
embedding = word_vectors['king']
print(embedding)
```

4. Positional Encoding: Transformers lack inherent information about the order of tokens in a sequence. To

address this, positional encoding is added to the embeddings. It provides information about the position of each token in the sequence, allowing the model to understand word order.

```python
# Positional encoding for Transformer models
import numpy as np

def positional_encoding(seq_len, embedding_dim):
    position = np.arange(0, seq_len).reshape(-1, 1)
    div_term = np.exp(np.arange(0, embedding_dim,
2) * -(np.log(10000.0) / embedding_dim))
    pos_enc = np.zeros((seq_len, embedding_dim))
    pos_enc[:, 0::2] = np.sin(position * div_term)
    pos_enc[:, 1::2] = np.cos(position * div_term)
    return pos_enc

seq_len = 10
embedding_dim = 512
pos_enc = positional_encoding(seq_len,
embedding_dim)
```

Padding:

5. Variable-Length Sequences: Text data often consists of variable-length sequences, which can be problematic for neural networks. Transformers, however, require fixed-size input.

6. Padding: Padding is the process of adding special tokens (usually with ID 0) to sequences to make them uniform in length. This ensures that all input sequences have the same dimensions, allowing for efficient batch processing during training.

```
# Padding sequences using TensorFlow
import tensorflow as tf

# Sample sequences
sequences = [[1, 2, 3], [4, 5], [6, 7, 8, 9]]

# Pad sequences to a maximum length
padded_sequences =
tf.keras.preprocessing.sequence.pad_sequences(seque
nces, maxlen=5, padding='post', truncating='post')
print(padded_sequences)
```

Output:

```
array([[1, 2, 3, 0, 0],
    [4, 5, 0, 0, 0],
    [6, 7, 8, 9, 0]], dtype=int32)
```

Data encoding and padding are essential for ensuring that text data is ready for processing by Transformer models. These steps enable the model to understand the content and structure of text while maintaining consistent input dimensions. Proper encoding methods and padding techniques contribute significantly to the effectiveness of Transformer-based NLP tasks.

2.4. Data Augmentation

Data augmentation is a crucial technique in Natural Language Processing (NLP) that helps enhance the diversity and size of your training dataset. By generating new training examples from your existing data, you can improve the generalization and robustness of your Transformer models. Let's explore data augmentation in detail:

What is Data Augmentation?

Data augmentation involves applying various transformations or modifications to your original data to create new instances while preserving the original label or meaning. In NLP, data augmentation can be particularly effective in scenarios with limited training data.

Common Data Augmentation Techniques:

1. Synonym Replacement: Replace words in the text with their synonyms while keeping the overall meaning intact. This helps expose the model to different word choices.

   Example:
   - Original: "The cat chased the mouse."
   - Augmented: "The feline pursued the rodent."

2. Back-Translation: Translate text from the target language back to the source language. This creates new, slightly varied sentences while preserving the original context.

Example:
- Original: "Je suis content." (French - "I am happy.")
- Back-Translation: "I am glad."

3. Random Deletion: Randomly remove words from a sentence. This forces the model to focus on the remaining words and understand context better.

Example:
- Original: "The quick brown fox jumps over the lazy dog."
- Augmented: "The brown fox jumps over the lazy dog."

4. Text Paraphrasing: Rewrite sentences with similar meaning but different phrasing. This introduces variations in sentence structure.

Example:
- Original: "The weather is pleasant today."

- Augmented: "Today's weather is nice."

5. Text Masking: Mask certain words or phrases in the text, simulating incomplete or noisy data. The model learns to fill in the gaps.

   Example:
   - Original: "The [MASK] is on the table."
   - Augmented: "The book is on the table."

Benefits of Data Augmentation:

1. Improved Generalization: Data augmentation exposes the model to a wider range of linguistic variations, making it more robust to different writing styles, sentence structures, and word choices.

2. Enhanced Performance: Models trained on augmented data often outperform those trained on limited original data, especially in low-resource settings.

3. Reduced Overfitting: Augmentation can help reduce overfitting by providing more diverse examples for the model to learn from.

Challenges and Considerations:

1. Semantic Integrity: While data augmentation is valuable, it's crucial to ensure that augmented data maintains the semantic integrity of the original text.

2. Label Preservation: When applying data augmentation, ensure that the labels or annotations associated with the original data remain accurate for the augmented samples.

3. Data Balance: Be mindful of maintaining a balanced dataset. Over-augmentation can lead to an imbalance in class distributions, affecting model performance.

Data augmentation is a powerful tool in your NLP toolkit, enabling you to make the most of your existing data. By generating diverse training examples, you can improve the performance and adaptability of your Transformer models, particularly in scenarios where large labeled datasets are scarce.

2.5. Dataset Splitting

Dataset splitting is a fundamental step in preparing your data for training and evaluating Transformer models in Natural Language Processing (NLP). It involves dividing your dataset into distinct subsets for training, validation, and testing. Let's explore dataset splitting in detail:

Why Dataset Splitting Matters:

1. Training: The training set is used to train your Transformer model. The model learns from this data and adjusts its parameters to make predictions.

2. Validation: The validation set is used to fine-tune model hyperparameters and monitor its performance during training. It helps you avoid overfitting by providing an independent evaluation.

3. Testing: The test set is reserved for the final evaluation of your model's performance. It serves as an unbiased assessment of how well your model generalizes to unseen data.

Common Dataset Splitting Strategies:

1. Random Splitting: This strategy randomly shuffles your data and assigns a portion to each subset. It's commonly used when you have a large and diverse dataset.

2. Stratified Splitting: Stratified splitting is used when you want to ensure that the class distribution in each subset mirrors the original dataset. This is crucial for imbalanced datasets.

Splitting Ratios:

The choice of splitting ratios depends on your dataset size and the specific goals of your NLP project. Common ratios include:

- 70-80% training, 10-15% validation, 10-15% testing for medium-sized datasets.
- 90% training, 5% validation, 5% testing for larger datasets.
- Adjust the ratios based on the size and characteristics of your dataset.

Implementation with Python:

In Python, libraries like `scikit-learn` provide convenient tools for dataset splitting.

```
from sklearn.model_selection import train_test_split

# Splitting into training, validation, and test sets
X_train, X_temp, y_train, y_temp =
train_test_split(X, y, test_size=0.3,
random_state=42)
X_val, X_test, y_val, y_test =
train_test_split(X_temp, y_temp, test_size=0.5,
random_state=42)

# X_train, y_train: Training data and labels.
# X_val, y_val: Validation data and labels.
```

X_test, y_test: Test data and labels.

Considerations:

1. Random Seed: Setting a random seed (e.g., `random_state` in scikit-learn) ensures reproducibility, as it generates the same split every time you run the code.

2. Stratification: If your dataset has class imbalance, use stratified splitting to ensure that each subset represents the class distribution accurately.

3. Cross-Validation: In addition to the train-validation-test split, consider using k-fold cross-validation, especially for smaller datasets. It provides more robust performance estimates.

4. Data Preprocessing: Perform data preprocessing (e.g., tokenization, data augmentation) before splitting to ensure consistency across subsets.

Dataset splitting is a critical aspect of NLP model development. It allows you to train, fine-tune, and evaluate your Transformer models in a systematic and unbiased manner. Proper splitting strategies and ratios are key to obtaining reliable performance estimates and building robust NLP solutions.

Chapter 3: Building Transformer Models

In this chapter, we will explore the process of building Transformer models for Natural Language Processing (NLP) tasks. We will cover various aspects of model architecture, implementation, and customization to suit your specific needs:

3.1. Model Architecture Choices

Selecting the appropriate Transformer model architecture is a critical decision in building Transformer-based solutions for Natural Language Processing (NLP) tasks. Let's explore the considerations and choices in model architecture:

1. Architecture Selection:

- BERT (Bidirectional Encoder Representations from Transformers): BERT is known for its bidirectional context understanding. It has revolutionized NLP by pretraining on massive text corpora and fine-tuning for downstream tasks. BERT variants include base, large, and more specialized models.

- GPT (Generative Pretrained Transformer): GPT models are autoregressive language models, trained to generate text. They are widely used for text generation tasks and can be fine-tuned for various NLP tasks.

- T5 (Text-to-Text Transfer Transformer): T5 models follow a unified "text-to-text" framework, where input and output are both treated as text. They are versatile and can be fine-tuned for different NLP tasks.

2. Model Size:

- Base vs. Large: Transformer models come in different sizes, typically categorized as base, large, or even extra-large. Larger models have more parameters and capacity but require more computational resources for training and inference. Choose a size that aligns with your dataset size and hardware capabilities.

3. Multi-Modal Transformers:

- Vision Transformers (ViTs): Transformers aren't limited to text. Vision Transformers apply the Transformer architecture to image data, making them suitable for tasks like image classification and object detection.

- Audio Transformers: Similar to ViTs, Transformers can be adapted for audio data, enabling applications like speech recognition and audio generation.

Code Example - Loading a Pre Trained BERT Model:

```
from transformers import BertTokenizer, BertModel

# Load the pretrained BERT tokenizer and model
tokenizer =
BertTokenizer.from_pretrained('bert-base-uncased')
model =
BertModel.from_pretrained('bert-base-uncased')
```

```
# Encode text and obtain embeddings
text = "Transformer models are powerful."
inputs = tokenizer(text, return_tensors="pt")
outputs = model(inputs)
embeddings = outputs.last_hidden_state

# embeddings contains contextual embeddings for
each token in the input
```

When choosing a model architecture, consider your specific NLP task, dataset size, available resources, and the trade-off between model size and performance. Many pretrained models are available, and fine-tuning them on your task can save significant time and resources. Experimentation and evaluation are key to determining the best architecture for your NLP project.

3.2. Implementing Transformers from Scratch

Implementing Transformers from scratch is an educational and insightful exercise that helps you understand the inner workings of these powerful models. In this section, we'll guide you through the key components of a basic Transformer model:

Building Blocks of Transformers:

1. Self-Attention Mechanism:

    - The self-attention mechanism is at the heart of Transformers. It allows each word in a sequence to focus on other words, capturing contextual information efficiently.

    - Implement self-attention using matrix operations, including queries, keys, and values.

2. Positional Encoding:

    - Transformers lack inherent knowledge of word order, so positional encoding is added to embeddings to provide positional information.

    - Use sinusoidal functions or learnable embeddings to encode positions.

3. Multi-Head Attention:

  - Multi-head attention enables the model to focus on different parts of the input sequence simultaneously.

  - Implement multiple sets of self-attention mechanisms, known as attention heads.

4. Feedforward Neural Networks (FFN):

  - Each Transformer layer includes a feedforward neural network. It applies linear transformations and activation functions to process attention outputs.

  - Implement a simple feedforward network with multiple layers.

5. Layer Normalization:

  - Layer normalization is applied to stabilize training by ensuring consistent input distributions across layers.

  - Implement layer normalization after each sublayer (attention and FFN).

Coding a Basic Transformer:

Below is a simplified Python example of a Transformer model. Note that this code is for educational purposes and doesn't include all optimizations found in production-ready Transformers:

```python
import torch
import torch.nn as nn

class TransformerLayer(nn.Module):
    def __init__(self, d_model, nhead):
        super(TransformerLayer, self).__init__()
        self.self_attention = nn.MultiheadAttention(d_model, nhead)
        self.layer_norm1 = nn.LayerNorm(d_model)
        self.feed_forward = nn.Sequential(
            nn.Linear(d_model, 2048),
            nn.ReLU(),
            nn.Linear(2048, d_model)
        )
        self.layer_norm2 = nn.LayerNorm(d_model)

    def forward(self, x):
        attn_output, _ = self.self_attention(x, x, x)
        x = x + attn_output
        x = self.layer_norm1(x)
```

```python
    ffn_output = self.feed_forward(x)
    x = x + ffn_output
    x = self.layer_norm2(x)
    return x

class Transformer(nn.Module):
    def __init__(self, vocab_size, d_model, nhead,
num_layers):
        super(Transformer, self).__init__()
        self.embedding = nn.Embedding(vocab_size,
d_model)
        self.layers =
nn.ModuleList([TransformerLayer(d_model, nhead)
for _ in range(num_layers)])

    def forward(self, x):
        x = self.embedding(x)
        for layer in self.layers:
            x = layer(x)
        return x

# Usage example
vocab_size = 10000
```

```
d_model = 512
nhead = 8
num_layers = 6

model = Transformer(vocab_size, d_model, nhead,
num_layers)
input_sequence = torch.randint(0, vocab_size, (10,
32))  # 10 words, batch size 32
output = model(input_sequence)
```

This code provides a simplified view of how to construct a Transformer model from scratch using PyTorch. In practice, state-of-the-art models are much more complex and optimized, but this example captures the core components of a Transformer for educational purposes.

Implementing Transformers from scratch is a valuable learning experience and can deepen your understanding of the inner workings of these models, helping you appreciate the innovations in modern NLP.

3.3. Utilizing Pretrained Transformer Models

Leveraging pretrained Transformer models is a game-changer in the world of Natural Language Processing (NLP). These models, pretrained on vast text corpora, capture extensive linguistic knowledge. Here's a comprehensive guide on how to utilize them effectively:

1. Pretrained Transformer Models:

- BERT (Bidirectional Encoder Representations from Transformers): BERT models are pre trained using a masked language modeling task. They learn to predict masked words in a sentence, forcing them to understand bidirectional context.

- GPT (Generative Pretrained Transformer): GPT models are pre trained as autoregressive language models. They predict the next word in a sequence, enabling them to generate coherent text.

- T5 (Text-to-Text Transfer Transformer): T5 models use a unified "text-to-text" framework where input and output are both treated as text. This versatility allows them to be fine-tuned for various NLP tasks.

2. Benefits of Pretrained Models:

- Transfer Learning: Pretrained models can be fine-tuned for specific downstream tasks, saving time and resources compared to training from scratch.

- Contextual Representations: Pretrained models provide contextual word embeddings, allowing them to capture the meaning of words based on their context.

- State-of-the-Art Performance: Pretrained models often achieve state-of-the-art results on various NLP benchmarks.

3. Using Hugging Face Transformers Library:

- The [Hugging Face Transformers](https://huggingface.co/transformers/) library is a powerful resource for working with pretrained models. It provides easy access to a wide range of pretrained models, including BERT, GPT, and more.

Example - Fine-Tuning a Pretrained BERT Model:

```
from transformers import BertTokenizer,
BertForSequenceClassification, AdamW
import torch

# Load pretrained BERT model and tokenizer
model_name = 'bert-base-uncased'
tokenizer =
BertTokenizer.from_pretrained(model_name)
model =
BertForSequenceClassification.from_pretrained(mod
el_name)

# Prepare data (you would have your own dataset)
text = ["This is a positive sentence.", "This is a
negative sentence."]
```

```
labels = [1, 0]
inputs = tokenizer(text, padding=True,
truncation=True, return_tensors="pt")

# Fine-tune BERT on your specific task
optimizer = AdamW(model.parameters(), lr=1e-5)
outputs = model(inputs,
labels=torch.tensor(labels).unsqueeze(0))
loss = outputs.loss
loss.backward()
optimizer.step()
```

4. Downstream Task Fine-Tuning:

- Fine-tuning pretrained models for specific tasks involves replacing the classification head with one suitable for your task (e.g., text classification, named entity recognition).

5. Model Evaluation and Inference:

- After fine-tuning, evaluate your model's performance on validation and test datasets using metrics relevant to your task (e.g., accuracy, F1-score).

- Use the fine-tuned model for inference on new data to make predictions or generate text.

6. Model Selection and Hyperparameter Tuning:

- Experiment with different pretrained models and architectures to find the one that suits your task best.

- Perform hyperparameter tuning, adjusting learning rates, batch sizes, and other training parameters to optimize model performance.

Utilizing pretrained Transformer models and libraries like Hugging Face Transformers can significantly accelerate your NLP projects. By fine-tuning these models on your specific tasks, you can harness their language understanding capabilities and achieve remarkable results with less effort compared to training from scratch.

3.4. Model Fine-Tuning and Customization

Fine-tuning and customization are essential steps when working with pre-trained Transformer models in Natural Language Processing (NLP). These processes allow you to adapt a general-purpose model to your specific task or domain. Here's a comprehensive guide on how to fine-tune and customize Transformer models:

1. Fine-Tuning Pretrained Models:

- Task-Specific Heads: When fine-tuning, you typically replace the classification head of the pretrained model with one suited to your specific task, such as text classification, named entity recognition, or sentiment analysis.

- Dataset Preparation: Prepare your task-specific dataset, ensuring it aligns with the model's input requirements. Tokenize the text, create input tensors, and organize labels accordingly.

- Hyperparameter Tuning: Experiment with hyperparameters like learning rate, batch size, and training epochs to optimize model performance on your task. Tools like learning rate schedules and early stopping can be valuable.

- Transfer Learning Benefits: Fine-tuning leverages the rich knowledge pretrained models have acquired from vast corpora, allowing you to achieve better results with smaller training datasets.

2. Customizing Transformer Architectures:

- Task-Specific Architectures: For some tasks, it's beneficial to customize the architecture of pretrained models. This can include modifying the number of layers, the size of hidden dimensions, or adding task-specific modules.

- Model Depth: Adjusting the number of layers or attention heads can control the model's capacity. Smaller models may be suitable for simpler tasks, while larger models can handle more complex ones.

- Positional Encoding: Depending on your task, you may need to customize the positional encoding scheme to better capture the sequence structure in your data.

3. Evaluation and Validation:

- Validation Set: Split your dataset into training, validation, and test sets. Use the validation set to monitor model performance during training and adjust hyperparameters.

- Performance Metrics: Choose appropriate evaluation metrics for your task, such as accuracy, F1-score, or mean squared error, to measure how well the model is performing.

4. Domain Adaptation:

- Domain-Specific Data: If your task involves a specific domain (e.g., medical, legal), consider fine-tuning on domain-specific data to improve model performance in that domain.

5. Handling Imbalanced Data:

- Class Imbalance: For tasks with imbalanced classes, employ techniques like class weighting, oversampling, or undersampling to address this issue.

6. Regularization Techniques:

- Dropout: Regularization techniques like dropout can help prevent overfitting by randomly dropping out neurons during training.

7. Batch Size Considerations:

- Batch Size: Adjusting the batch size can impact training dynamics. Smaller batch sizes may provide more stable gradients, while larger batch sizes can lead to faster convergence.

8. Experimentation and Iteration:

- Iterative Process: Fine-tuning and customization often require experimentation and multiple iterations to achieve the best results. Be prepared to adjust parameters and strategies based on performance feedback.

- Monitoring Progress: Continuously monitor training progress, visualize loss curves, and inspect model predictions to diagnose issues and make improvements.

9. Inference and Deployment:

- Inference: After fine-tuning, use the model for inference on new data. Ensure that your inference pipeline includes tokenization and data preprocessing steps.

- Deployment: Deploy your fine-tuned model to a production environment, whether on the cloud, edge devices, or servers, to make predictions at scale.

Fine-tuning and customization allow you to harness the power of pretrained Transformer models while tailoring them to your specific NLP tasks and domains. By following best practices in model evaluation, hyperparameter tuning, and domain adaptation, you can achieve state-of-the-art results and build robust NLP solutions.

Chapter 4: Training and Optimization

In Chapter 4, we will deal with the crucial aspects of training and optimizing Transformer models for Natural Language Processing (NLP). These topics are essential for achieving good model performance and ensuring that your models generalize well:

4.1. Loss Functions

Loss functions are a fundamental component of training machine learning models, including Transformer models for Natural Language Processing (NLP). They quantify the difference between predicted and actual values, guiding the model towards optimal parameters during training. Let's explore common loss functions used in NLP and how to choose the right one for your task:

1. Cross-Entropy Loss (Log Loss):

- Use Cases: Cross-entropy loss is the standard choice for classification tasks. It measures the dissimilarity between predicted class probabilities and true class labels.

- Mathematical Formulation:
  - For binary classification:
    - $L(y, \hat{y}) = - [y * \log(\hat{y}) + (1 - y) * \log(1 - \hat{y})]$
  - For multiclass classification (C classes):
    - $L(y, \hat{y}) = - \Sigma(y\_i * \log(\hat{y}\_i))$

2. Mean Squared Error (MSE) Loss:

- Use Cases: MSE loss is commonly used for regression tasks, where the model predicts continuous values. It measures the average squared difference between predicted and actual values.

- Mathematical Formulation:
  - $L(y, \hat{y}) = \Sigma(y\_i - \hat{y}\_i)^2 / N$

3. Custom Loss Functions:

- Use Cases: In some cases, predefined loss functions may not suit your specific task. You can create custom loss functions tailored to your problem domain.

- Implementation Example (PyTorch):

```python
import torch.nn as nn

class CustomLoss(nn.Module):
    def __init__(self, weight):
        super(CustomLoss, self).__init__()
        self.weight = weight

    def forward(self, y_pred, y_true):
        loss = self.weight * (y_pred -
y_true).pow(2).mean()
        return loss
```

Choosing the Right Loss Function:

- Classification vs. Regression: Choose cross-entropy loss for classification tasks and mean squared error loss for regression tasks.

- Multiclass vs. Binary Classification: Use cross-entropy loss with a single sigmoid output for binary classification and softmax output for multiclass classification.

- Imbalanced Datasets: For imbalanced datasets, consider using weighted loss functions to give more importance to minority classes.

Example - Using Cross-Entropy Loss (PyTorch):

```python
import torch
import torch.nn as nn
import torch.optim as optim

# Define a simple binary classification model
class BinaryClassifier(nn.Module):
    def __init__(self):
        super(BinaryClassifier, self).__init__()
        self.fc = nn.Linear(10, 1)

    def forward(self, x):
        return torch.sigmoid(self.fc(x))
```

```python
# Instantiate the model and define loss function
model = BinaryClassifier()
criterion = nn.BCELoss()  # Binary Cross-Entropy Loss

# Generate some example data
X = torch.randn(100, 10)
y = torch.randint(0, 2, (100, 1), dtype=torch.float32)

# Define optimizer
optimizer = optim.Adam(model.parameters(), lr=0.001)

# Training loop
for epoch in range(100):
    optimizer.zero_grad()
    outputs = model(X)
    loss = criterion(outputs, y)
    loss.backward()
    optimizer.step()
```

Choosing the appropriate loss function is crucial for training your Transformer models effectively. Consider the nature of your NLP task, the data type of your target variable, and whether you need to handle class imbalances when selecting a loss function.

4.2. Gradient Descent and Optimizers

Gradient descent and optimizers are fundamental components of training deep learning models, including Transformer models for Natural Language Processing (NLP). They dictate how model parameters are updated during training to minimize the loss function. Here's a comprehensive guide to understanding gradient descent and optimizers:

1. Gradient Descent:

- Objective: The primary objective of training a machine learning model is to find the model parameters that minimize a defined loss function.

- Gradient Descent: Gradient descent is an iterative optimization algorithm used to find the minimum of a function, often the loss function in machine learning. It works by iteratively adjusting model parameters in the direction of the steepest descent (negative gradient) of the loss function.

- Mathematical Formulation:
  - θ represents the model parameters (weights and biases).
  - α (learning rate) controls the step size in each iteration.

  Update Rule: $\theta\_new = \theta\_old - \alpha * \nabla L(\theta\_old)$

2. Optimizers:

- Challenges: Gradient descent can be slow and may suffer from convergence issues in practice. Optimizers address these challenges by enhancing the optimization process.

- Popular Optimizers:

- Stochastic Gradient Descent (SGD): Basic optimizer that updates parameters based on the gradient of the entire training dataset or a mini-batch.

- Adam (Adaptive Moment Estimation): Combines elements of momentum and RMSprop. It adapts learning rates for each parameter individually.

- RMSprop (Root Mean Square Propagation): Maintains a moving average of squared gradients to adjust the learning rates.

3. Learning Rate:

- Importance: The learning rate (α) determines the step size during each parameter update. It's a critical hyperparameter that can significantly impact training.

- Tuning: Choosing an appropriate learning rate is often an iterative process. Too high a learning rate may lead to overshooting the minimum, while too low a learning rate can slow down convergence.

4. Mini-Batch Gradient Descent:

- Advantage: Training on the entire dataset (batch gradient descent) can be computationally expensive. Mini-batch gradient descent divides the dataset into smaller batches, allowing for faster convergence and better generalization.

5. Momentum and Accelerated Optimization:

- Momentum: Optimizers like Adam incorporate momentum to help overcome local minima by smoothing out parameter updates.

- Acceleration: Techniques like Nesterov Accelerated Gradient (NAG) further enhance convergence by considering the "lookahead" gradient.

6. Adaptive Learning Rates:

- Adaptive Optimizers: Adam and RMSprop are adaptive optimizers that automatically adjust learning rates for each parameter based on the history of gradient updates.

7. Hyperparameter Tuning:

- Grid Search or Random Search: Hyperparameter tuning is often done using grid search or random search to find the combination of learning rate, optimizer, and other hyperparameters that result in the best model performance.

8. Stopping Criteria:

- Early Stopping: Training is usually stopped when performance on a validation set plateaus or starts deteriorating, preventing overfitting.

Understanding gradient descent and choosing the right optimizer and learning rate are pivotal for training successful Transformer models. These techniques ensure that the model converges to an optimal solution while avoiding common issues like slow convergence or overshooting. Experimentation and careful tuning are often necessary to achieve the best results.

4.3. Learning Rate Scheduling

Learning rate scheduling is a critical technique in training deep learning models, including Transformers for Natural Language Processing (NLP). It involves adjusting the learning rate during training to improve convergence and model performance. Here's a comprehensive guide to understanding learning rate scheduling:

1. The Role of Learning Rate:

- Learning Rate (α): Learning rate determines the size of steps taken in the gradient descent optimization process. It's a crucial hyperparameter as it impacts how quickly the model converges and whether it reaches an optimal solution.

- Challenges with Fixed Learning Rates: Using a fixed learning rate throughout training can lead to issues such as slow convergence, overshooting, or getting stuck in local minima.

2. Learning Rate Scheduling Techniques:

- Learning Rate Annealing: Learning rate annealing involves gradually reducing the learning rate during training. It can be done using various strategies:

  - Step Decay: Decrease the learning rate by a fixed factor (e.g., 0.1) after a fixed number of epochs.
    - Exponential Decay: Reduce the learning rate exponentially over time.
  - Cosine Annealing: Vary the learning rate following a cosine function, which results in a cyclical learning rate schedule.

3. Benefits of Learning Rate Scheduling:

- Faster Convergence: Learning rate scheduling allows the model to start with a larger learning rate for faster convergence in the initial training stages.

- Fine-Tuning: It enables the model to fine-tune its parameters with a smaller learning rate, helping it settle into a better local minimum.

- Robustness: Learning rate scheduling can make training more robust, helping models escape from saddle points and find better optima.

4. Learning Rate Scheduling in PyTorch:

- PyTorch provides learning rate scheduling as part of its training utilities. Here's an example of how to implement learning rate scheduling using PyTorch:

```
import torch.optim as optim
from torch.optim.lr_scheduler import StepLR

# Define optimizer and learning rate scheduler
optimizer = optim.Adam(model.parameters(),
lr=0.001)
scheduler = StepLR(optimizer, step_size=10,
gamma=0.5)  # Adjust learning rate every 10 epochs

# Training loop with learning rate scheduling
for epoch in range(100):
    optimizer.zero_grad()
```

```
    # Forward pass, loss computation, and backward
pass here
    optimizer.step()
    scheduler.step()  # Update learning rate

# Learning rate will be reduced by a factor of 0.5
every 10 epochs
```

5. Choosing the Right Learning Rate Schedule:

- Problem-Specific: The choice of learning rate schedule can be problem-specific. Experiment with different schedules and see which one works best for your task.

- Monitoring: Continuously monitor model performance during training to ensure the learning rate schedule is helping convergence.

6. Other Techniques: Learning rate scheduling can be combined with other techniques like warm-up steps (gradually increasing the learning rate at the beginning) or cyclic learning rate schedules for more advanced optimization.

Learning rate scheduling is a valuable tool for improving the training of Transformer models. By adapting the learning rate over time, you can achieve faster convergence, better optima, and more robust training dynamics. Experimentation is key to finding the most effective learning rate schedule for your specific NLP task.

4.4. Overfitting and Regularization

Overfitting is a common challenge in training deep learning models, including Transformers for Natural Language Processing (NLP). Regularization techniques are essential to combat overfitting and improve model generalization. Here's an extensive guide to understanding overfitting and regularization:

1. Overfitting:

- Definition: Overfitting occurs when a model performs exceptionally well on the training data but poorly on unseen or validation data. It indicates that the model has memorized the training data rather than learned to generalize.

- Causes: Overfitting can result from a model having too many parameters relative to the size of the training dataset, which allows it to fit noise or irrelevant patterns.

2. Regularization Techniques:

Regularization methods introduce constraints or penalties to the model during training, discouraging it from fitting the training data too closely.

3. L1 and L2 Regularization:

- L1 Regularization (Lasso): L1 adds the absolute values of the model's weights to the loss function. It encourages sparse weight matrices, effectively driving some features to zero.

- L2 Regularization (Ridge): L2 adds the squared values of the model's weights to the loss function. It discourages large weights and helps prevent extreme parameter values.

4. Dropout:

- Dropout: Dropout is a regularization technique where randomly selected neurons (or weights) are "dropped out" during training. It prevents the model from relying too heavily on specific neurons, thus reducing overfitting.

5. Early Stopping:

- Early Stopping: Monitor model performance on a validation set during training. If the performance plateaus or starts to deteriorate, stop training to prevent overfitting.

6. Data Augmentation:

- Data Augmentation: Increase the effective size of your training dataset by applying random transformations to the input data, such as rotation, cropping, or adding noise.

7. Weight Constraints:

- Weight Constraints: Limit the magnitude of weights during training to prevent them from growing too large. This can be achieved by setting weight bounds.

8. Batch Normalization:

- Batch Normalization: Batch normalization can stabilize training by normalizing activations within each mini-batch. It acts as a form of implicit regularization.

9. Hyperparameter Tuning:

- Hyperparameter Tuning: Experiment with regularization hyperparameters like the strength of L1 and L2 regularization, dropout rates, and batch normalization parameters to find the optimal values for your model and task.

Example - L2 Regularization in PyTorch:

```
import torch
```

```python
import torch.nn as nn
import torch.optim as optim

# Define a simple neural network with L2
regularization
class NeuralNetwork(nn.Module):
    def __init__(self, input_size, hidden_size,
output_size, l2_lambda):
        super(NeuralNetwork, self).__init__()
        self.fc1 = nn.Linear(input_size, hidden_size)
        self.relu = nn.ReLU()
        self.fc2 = nn.Linear(hidden_size, output_size)
        self.l2_lambda = l2_lambda  # Regularization
strength

    def forward(self, x):
        x = self.fc1(x)
        x = self.relu(x)
        x = self.fc2(x)
        return x

# Instantiate the model and optimizer with L2
regularization
```

```
input_size = 100
hidden_size = 50
output_size = 10
l2_lambda = 0.01  # Regularization strength
model = NeuralNetwork(input_size, hidden_size,
output_size, l2_lambda)
optimizer = optim.Adam(model.parameters(),
lr=0.001, weight_decay=l2_lambda)  # Weight decay
applies L2 regularization

# Training loop with L2 regularization
for epoch in range(100):
    optimizer.zero_grad()
    # Forward pass, loss computation, and backward
pass here
    optimizer.step()
```

Regularization techniques are indispensable for preventing overfitting and ensuring your Transformer models generalize well to unseen data. By carefully selecting and tuning these techniques, you can build models that strike the right balance between fitting the training data and generalizing to new inputs.

4.5. Training Best Practices

Training Transformer models for Natural Language Processing (NLP) requires a set of best practices to ensure efficient convergence, robustness, and optimal model performance. Here are key practices to follow:

1. Data Preprocessing:

- Data Cleaning: Clean and preprocess your dataset by removing noise, handling missing values, and ensuring data consistency.

- Tokenization: Tokenize text data into subword units (e.g., BPE, WordPiece) using appropriate tokenizers like those provided by the Hugging Face Transformers library.

- Vocabulary: Build a vocabulary of tokens and handle out-of-vocabulary (OOV) words appropriately.

2. Data Augmentation:

- Augmentation Techniques: Apply data augmentation methods to increase the effective size of your training dataset. Techniques include paraphrasing, back-translation, and adding noise.

3. Handling Imbalanced Data:

- Class Imbalance: Address class imbalance in classification tasks by using techniques like class weighting, oversampling, or undersampling.

4. Model Initialization:

- Pretrained Models: Start with pre-trained Transformer models (e.g., BERT, GPT) as they provide valuable contextual embeddings and can significantly boost performance.

5. Learning Rate and Optimizers:

- Learning Rate Scheduling: Implement learning rate scheduling to adjust the learning rate during training. Common schedules include step decay and cosine annealing.

- Optimizer Choice: Experiment with different optimizers (e.g., Adam, SGD) and monitor how they affect convergence and performance.

6. Mini-Batch Training:

- Mini-Batches: Train your model on mini-batches of data rather than the entire dataset. This speeds up convergence and reduces memory requirements.

- Batch Size: Choose an appropriate batch size based on available memory and hardware capabilities. Larger batch sizes often lead to more stable gradients.

7. Regularization:

- Weight Decay: Apply weight decay (L2 regularization) to prevent large weights. This is especially important for preventing overfitting in deep models.

- Dropout: Use dropout layers to prevent overfitting by randomly dropping out neurons during training.

8. Early Stopping:

- Validation Monitoring: Monitor your model's performance on a validation set during training. Implement early stopping to prevent overfitting when performance plateaus or deteriorates.

9. Model Evaluation:

- Metrics: Use appropriate evaluation metrics for your task (e.g., accuracy, F1-score, perplexity) to measure how well your model is performing.

- Validation and Test Sets: Split your data into training, validation, and test sets. Validate your model on the validation set and evaluate its final performance on the test set.

10. Hyperparameter Tuning:

- Grid Search or Random Search: Systematically search for optimal hyperparameters like learning rate, dropout rates, and model architecture using grid search or random search.

11. Monitoring Training:

- Loss Curves: Visualize training loss curves to ensure convergence. Monitor the progression of loss on both training and validation sets.

- Learning Rate: Keep track of learning rate changes and their impact on training dynamics.

12. GPU Acceleration:

- Utilize GPUs: If available, use GPUs for training as they significantly speed up model training.

13. Experimentation:

- Iterative Process: Training deep models often requires experimentation and multiple iterations. Be prepared to adjust parameters and strategies based on performance feedback.

14. Model Saving and Loading:

- Checkpointing: Save model checkpoints during training to resume training or perform inference later.

15. Documentation:

- Record Hyperparameters: Document the hyperparameters used for each experiment, making it easier to replicate or build upon your work.

16. Deployment Considerations:

- Model Export: Prepare your model for deployment by exporting it in a format compatible with your deployment environment (e.g., TensorFlow SavedModel, PyTorch Script Module).

By following these best practices, you can increase the chances of successfully training Transformer models for NLP tasks. Training deep learning models is often an iterative process that requires careful consideration of data, hyperparameters, and training strategies to achieve the best results.

Chapter 5: Applications of Transformers in NLP

In this chapter, we explore various practical applications of Transformer models in Natural Language Processing (NLP). These applications showcase the versatility and power of Transformers in understanding and generating human language:

5.1. Chatbots and Conversational AI

Chatbots and conversational AI systems powered by Transformers have emerged as powerful tools for natural language understanding and generation. They enable human-like interactions between users and machines, offering a wide range of applications and benefits:

1. Overview:

- Conversational AI: Conversational AI is the field of artificial intelligence focused on developing systems that can engage in meaningful, human-like conversations with users.

2. How Transformers Revolutionized Chatbots:

- Contextual Understanding: Transformers excel at contextual understanding due to their self-attention mechanisms. They can analyze and generate text based on the context of the conversation, making interactions more natural and context-aware.

- Large Pretrained Models: Pretrained models like GPT-3 and BERT have set new benchmarks in chatbot performance. These models, with billions of parameters, have impressive language understanding and generation capabilities.

3. Use Cases:

- Customer Support: Chatbots are commonly used in customer support to handle routine inquiries, answer frequently asked questions, and guide users through troubleshooting processes. They offer 24/7 availability and consistency in responses.

- Virtual Assistants: Virtual assistants like Siri, Alexa, and Google Assistant employ chatbot technology to perform tasks, answer questions, and control smart devices through voice or text interactions.

- E-commerce: Chatbots assist customers in finding products, providing product information, and processing orders. They enhance user experiences and drive sales.

- Social Media: Chatbots are used on social media platforms for various purposes, including automated responses, content recommendations, and personalized interactions.

4. Natural Language Generation:

- Contextual Responses: Transformers enable chatbots to generate responses that are contextually relevant to the conversation. They can understand and remember previous messages, leading to more engaging interactions.

- Personalization: Chatbots can personalize responses based on user preferences and history, creating a more tailored user experience.

5. Challenges:

- Open Domain vs. Domain-Specific: Developing chatbots that perform well in open-domain conversations, where users can discuss various topics, is challenging. Domain-specific chatbots, tailored for a specific task or industry, may have more focused but effective interactions.

- Ethical Concerns: Ensuring chatbots provide accurate and ethical responses is crucial. Preventing the spread of misinformation and addressing biases in language generation are ongoing challenges.

6. Multimodal Conversations:

- Beyond Text: Modern chatbots are evolving to support multimodal conversations that involve text, images, and even voice inputs. This enables richer interactions and better user experiences.

7. Future Trends:

- Multilingual Chatbots: Chatbots that can communicate in multiple languages are becoming increasingly important in our interconnected world.

- Conversational AI in Healthcare: Chatbots are being used for healthcare-related tasks such as appointment scheduling, symptom checking, and medication reminders.

- Voice Assistants: Voice-activated chatbots and virtual assistants are expected to play a more prominent role in our daily lives, especially in smart homes and cars.

Chatbots and conversational AI systems powered by Transformers have made significant strides in mimicking human-like interactions. As these technologies continue to advance, they will play pivotal roles in improving customer service, enhancing user experiences, and providing valuable assistance in various domains. However, ethical considerations and responsible development remain essential aspects of their continued growth.

5.2. Sentiment Analysis

Sentiment analysis, also known as opinion mining, is a natural language processing (NLP) technique that focuses on understanding and extracting the sentiment or emotional tone expressed in text. Sentiment analysis powered by Transformers has gained prominence due to its applications in various domains. Here's an in-depth exploration of sentiment analysis:

1. Overview:

- Sentiment Analysis: Sentiment analysis aims to determine the sentiment conveyed in a piece of text, such as positive, negative, or neutral. It can also go beyond these basic categories to detect specific emotions like joy, anger, or sadness.

2. How Transformers Enhance Sentiment Analysis:

- Contextual Understanding: Transformers excel at contextual understanding, allowing them to capture nuances in language and provide more accurate sentiment analysis results. They consider the surrounding words and phrases to determine sentiment.

- Large Pretrained Models: Pretrained models like BERT and GPT have extensive vocabularies and general language knowledge, making them effective at identifying sentiment cues.

3. Use Cases:

- Brand Monitoring: Companies use sentiment analysis to monitor social media, news articles, and customer reviews to gauge public sentiment about their products or services.

- Customer Feedback Analysis: Sentiment analysis helps businesses understand customer opinions, identify areas for improvement, and make data-driven decisions.

- Product Reviews: E-commerce platforms use sentiment analysis to classify product reviews as positive or negative, making it easier for customers to make purchasing decisions.

- Social Media Sentiment Trends: Social media platforms use sentiment analysis to track trends and user sentiment, which can inform content recommendations and advertising strategies.

4. Sentiment Classification:

- Binary Classification: In binary sentiment classification, text is categorized as either positive or negative. For example, determining whether a movie review is positive or negative.

- Multiclass Classification: Multiclass sentiment analysis assigns text to multiple sentiment categories, such as positive, neutral, and negative, or even specific emotions like joy, anger, or surprise.

5. Challenges:

- Ambiguity: Language can be highly ambiguous, and sentiment analysis models must disambiguate phrases or sentences to assign the correct sentiment.

- Context Matters: The same words can have different meanings in different contexts, requiring models to consider the broader context in which text appears.

- Irony and Sarcasm: Identifying irony and sarcasm is challenging for sentiment analysis models, as the sentiment expressed may be the opposite of the literal meaning.

6. Sentiment Lexicons and Datasets:

- Sentiment Lexicons: Sentiment analysis often uses sentiment lexicons or dictionaries containing words associated with positive or negative sentiment. Models reference these lexicons to analyze sentiment.

- Labeled Datasets: Training sentiment analysis models requires large labeled datasets with text examples and corresponding sentiment labels.

7. Fine-Tuning Transformers:

- Transfer Learning: Fine-tuning pretrained Transformers is a common approach in sentiment analysis. Models like BERT are pre trained on vast text corpora and can be fine-tuned on smaller datasets for specific sentiment analysis tasks.

8. Future Trends:

- Multimodal Sentiment Analysis: Sentiment analysis is expanding to analyze sentiment in images, audio, and videos, enabling a more comprehensive understanding of user sentiment.

- Domain-Specific Sentiment Analysis: Custom sentiment analysis models tailored to specific industries or domains (e.g., healthcare, finance) are becoming more prevalent.

- Ethical Considerations: Ensuring that sentiment analysis models do not exhibit biases and accurately represent diverse voices is an ongoing concern in the field.

Sentiment analysis powered by Transformers has become a valuable tool for businesses, marketers, and researchers to gain insights into public opinion and user sentiment. As the technology continues to advance, it will play a crucial role in improving decision-making processes and user experiences across various domains.

5.3. Machine Translation

Machine translation is the task of automatically translating text from one language to another. Transformers have revolutionized machine translation, leading to significant improvements in translation quality and fluency. Here's an in-depth look at machine translation with Transformers:

1. Overview:

- Machine Translation: Machine translation is the process of using algorithms and models to convert text or speech from one language (source) to another language (target) while preserving meaning.

2. How Transformers Revolutionized Machine Translation:

- Attention Mechanism: Transformers introduced the self-attention mechanism, which allows the model to weigh the importance of different words in the source and target languages. This mechanism captures contextual information, improving translation quality.

- Bidirectional Context: Transformers can consider both preceding and following words, leading to better contextual understanding. This bidirectional context is crucial for translating languages with different word orders and structures.

3. Use Cases:

- Global Communication: Machine translation enables people from different linguistic backgrounds to communicate effectively. It's widely used for emails, social media, and online chats.

- E-commerce: E-commerce platforms use machine translation to provide product information and customer support in multiple languages, expanding their global reach.

- Content Localization: Content creators and businesses use machine translation to adapt websites, apps, and marketing materials for international audiences.

4. Challenges:

- Idioms and Culture: Machine translation struggles with idiomatic expressions, cultural nuances, and language-specific jokes. These elements often require human understanding.

- Low-Resource Languages: Some languages have limited training data, making it challenging to develop accurate translation models. Transformers can still help improve translation in these cases but may not achieve state-of-the-art results.

- Evaluation Metrics: Measuring translation quality accurately is complex. Metrics like BLEU, TER, and METEOR are commonly used but have limitations in assessing the naturalness and fluency of translations.

5. Neural Machine Translation:

- Sequence-to-Sequence Models: Neural machine translation models, including Transformer-based models, operate in a sequence-to-sequence manner. They transform input sequences (source language) into output sequences (target language).

6. Training Transformers for Translation:

- Pretraining: Transformers are pre trained on large text corpora in multiple languages to learn general language representations.

- Fine-Tuning: Fine-tuning is performed on translation-specific datasets, aligning source and target sentences to teach the model the translation task.

7. Multilingual Models:

- Multilingual Transformers: Some models, like mBERT (multilingual BERT), are pre trained on text from multiple languages. They can handle translation between a wide range of language pairs.

8. Low-Resource Languages:

- Transfer Learning: Transfer learning from high-resource to low-resource languages is a promising approach. Models pre-trained on widely spoken languages can be fine-tuned on limited data for less common languages.

9. Future Trends:

- Continuous Advancements: Transformers continue to evolve, and further improvements in translation quality are expected as models become larger and more sophisticated.

- Real-Time Translation: Real-time, on-device translation applications are becoming more common, allowing users to communicate seamlessly across languages in various contexts.

- Domain-Specific Translation: Customized translation models for specific domains (e.g., medical, legal) are expected to improve accuracy and fluency in specialized fields.

Machine translation powered by Transformers has made language barriers more permeable, facilitating global communication and access to information. While challenges remain, continued research and development in this field promise even more accurate and natural translations, benefiting individuals and businesses worldwide.

Chapter 6: Handling Real-World Data

In this chapter, we deal with the challenges and considerations when working with real-world data in Natural Language Processing (NLP) tasks. Addressing issues such as imbalanced data, noisy text, and ethical concerns is crucial for developing robust and responsible NLP solutions.

6.1. Dealing with Imbalanced Data

Handling imbalanced data is a critical aspect of machine learning, including Natural Language Processing (NLP). In imbalanced datasets, one class significantly outweighs the others, which can lead to biased models. Here's an in-depth exploration with code examples on how to address imbalanced data in NLP:

1. Imbalanced Data Overview:

Imbalanced data occurs when one class (the minority class) has far fewer examples than another class (the majority class) in a dataset. In NLP, this might mean having very few examples of rare sentiments or underrepresented categories.

2. Challenges of Imbalanced Data:

- Bias in Model Training: Imbalanced datasets can cause models to be biased towards the majority class, leading to poor performance on the minority class.

- Misleading Metrics: Accuracy is not a reliable metric when dealing with imbalanced data, as a model that predicts the majority class can still achieve high accuracy.

3. Strategies for Handling Imbalanced Data:

Resampling:

- Over-sampling: Over-sampling involves creating additional copies of minority class samples to balance the dataset. The Synthetic Minority Over-sampling Technique (SMOTE) generates synthetic examples.

```
from imblearn.over_sampling import SMOTE

# Create an instance of SMOTE
smote = SMOTE(sampling_strategy='auto',
random_state=42)

# Apply SMOTE to your data
X_resampled, y_resampled = smote.fit_resample(X,
y)
```

- Under-sampling: Under-sampling randomly removes instances from the majority class to balance the dataset.

```
from imblearn.under_sampling import
RandomUnderSampler

# Create an instance of RandomUnderSampler
rus =
RandomUnderSampler(sampling_strategy='auto',
random_state=42)
```

```
# Apply under-sampling to your data
X_resampled, y_resampled = rus.fit_resample(X, y)
```

Cost-Sensitive Learning:

- Assign different misclassification costs for different classes to make the model pay more attention to minority classes.

```
from sklearn.svm import SVC
```

```
# Create a model with class weights
model = SVC(class_weight='balanced')
model.fit(X_train, y_train)
```

Ensemble Methods:

- Ensemble methods like Random Forests or AdaBoost can combine predictions from multiple models.

```
from sklearn.ensemble import RandomForestClassifier
```

```
# Create a Random Forest Classifier with balanced
class weights
rf_model                                    =
RandomForestClassifier(class_weight='balanced',
random_state=42)
rf_model.fit(X_train, y_train)
```

4. Evaluation Metrics:

When working with imbalanced data, consider using evaluation metrics such as precision, recall, F1-score, and area under the Receiver Operating Characteristic curve (AUC-ROC) to assess model performance more effectively.

Handling imbalanced data in NLP requires a thoughtful approach, as it can significantly impact the quality of your machine learning models. These techniques and metrics can help you develop models that provide more equitable predictions across all classes, ultimately improving the utility of your NLP solutions.

6.2. Handling Noisy Text

Handling noisy text data is essential in Natural Language Processing (NLP) because real-world text often contains errors, misspellings, abbreviations, and non-standard language. Managing noisy text is crucial for improving the quality of NLP models. Here's an in-depth exploration with code examples on how to handle noisy text data:

1. Noisy Text Overview:

- Noisy Text: Noisy text refers to text data that contains various forms of errors and inconsistencies, such as typos, misspellings, grammatical errors, slang, abbreviations, and non-standard language usage.

2. Challenges of Noisy Text:

- Impact on Models: Noisy text can mislead NLP models, leading to incorrect predictions, sentiment analysis errors, or inaccurate translations.

- Loss of Interpretability: Noisy text can hinder the interpretability of NLP models, making it difficult to understand their decisions and reasoning.

3. Strategies for Handling Noisy Text:

Data Cleaning:

- Spell Checking: Correct misspelled words using spell-checking libraries like `pyspellchecker`.

```
from spellchecker import SpellChecker

spell = SpellChecker()
def correct_spelling(text):
    words = text.split()
    corrected_words = [spell.correction(word) for word in words]
    return ' '.join(corrected_words)

cleaned_text = correct_spelling(noisy_text)
```

- Lemmatization: Use lemmatization to reduce words to their base or dictionary form, which can help in noise reduction.

```
from nltk.stem import WordNetLemmatizer

lemmatizer = WordNetLemmatizer()
def lemmatize_text(text):
    words = text.split()
    lemmatized_words = [lemmatizer.lemmatize(word)
for word in words]
    return ' '.join(lemmatized_words)

cleaned_text = lemmatize_text(noisy_text)
```

Regularization Techniques:

- Dropout: Apply dropout during model training to reduce overfitting and make models more robust to noise.

```
from tensorflow.keras.layers import Dropout

model = Sequential()
```

```
model.add(Embedding(input_dim=vocab_size,
output_dim=embedding_dim,
input_length=max_length))
model.add(LSTM(64, return_sequences=True))
model.add(Dropout(0.2))
model.add(Dense(1, activation='sigmoid'))
```

- Weight Regularization: Use weight regularization techniques like L1 or L2 regularization to prevent model parameters from fitting to noise.

```
from tensorflow.keras.regularizers import l2

model = Sequential()
model.add(Dense(64, input_dim=input_dim,
kernel_regularizer=l2(0.01), activation='relu'))
model.add(Dense(1, activation='sigmoid'))
'''
```

Ensemble Models:

- Ensemble Methods: Combine predictions from multiple models to reduce the impact of noisy data.

```
from sklearn.ensemble import VotingClassifier

model1 = LogisticRegression()
model2 = RandomForestClassifier()
model3 = GradientBoostingClassifier()

ensemble_model = VotingClassifier(estimators=[('lr',
model1), ('rf', model2), ('gb', model3)], voting='soft')
ensemble_model.fit(X_train, y_train)
```

Handling noisy text in NLP is essential for building accurate and reliable models. By implementing data cleaning, regularization techniques, and ensemble methods, you can reduce the impact of noise and improve the overall performance and interpretability of your NLP models.

6.3. Ethical Considerations in Data Usage

Ethical considerations in data usage are of utmost importance in Natural Language Processing (NLP) and machine learning. As NLP models become increasingly powerful and influential, it's vital to address ethical concerns to ensure responsible and fair use of data. Here's an in-depth exploration of ethical considerations in data usage in NLP:

1. Data Bias and Fairness:

- Data Bias: Bias in training data can lead to biased NLP models. Biases may arise from historical inequalities, underrepresentation of certain groups, or biased annotations. For example, if a sentiment analysis dataset primarily contains reviews from a specific demographic, the model may not generalize well to other groups.

- Fairness: Ensuring fairness in NLP models means that predictions and decisions should not discriminate against specific demographic groups. Fairness metrics and bias detection techniques are used to identify and mitigate these issues.

2. Privacy Concerns:

- Sensitive Data: NLP models often process sensitive text data, such as medical records, personal conversations, or financial information. Handling this data must prioritize privacy and security.

- Privacy-Preserving Methods: Techniques like differential privacy and federated learning are used to protect sensitive data during model training and inference.

3. Transparency and Accountability:

- Transparency: AI developers should be transparent about how NLP models work, their limitations, and the data sources used. This transparency helps users understand and trust the technology.

- Explainability: Making NLP models interpretable and explainable is crucial for understanding their decision-making processes. Explainable AI techniques, such as attention maps, can help reveal which parts of the input data influenced the model's output.

- Accountability: Developers and organizations should take responsibility for the actions and consequences of their NLP models. This includes addressing errors, biases, and ethical concerns promptly.

4. Bias Detection and Mitigation:

- Bias Detection: Various tools and techniques are available to detect bias in NLP models and data. These include analyzing the demographic distribution of training data and evaluating model predictions for fairness.

- Bias Mitigation: Once bias is detected, mitigation strategies involve re-sampling data, fine-tuning models, or adjusting decision thresholds to reduce bias and ensure fair outcomes.

5. Ethical Guidelines and Standards:

- Industry Standards: Organizations like the IEEE and ACM have established ethical guidelines and standards for AI and NLP development. These guidelines help practitioners make ethical decisions throughout the development process.

6. Informed Consent:

- User Consent: When collecting text data from users, obtaining informed consent is essential. Users should understand how their data will be used, who will have access to it, and for what purposes.

- Data Anonymization: Anonymizing data, removing personally identifiable information, and using aggregated data when possible can protect user privacy.

7. Bias in Language Models:

- Dealing with Bias: Developers of large language models, like GPT-3, are actively addressing concerns about bias in model outputs, especially when models generate offensive or harmful content. Research and engineering efforts aim to reduce these biases.

8. Ongoing Evaluation and Improvement:

- Continuous Monitoring: Ethical considerations in NLP are not static; they evolve with technology and societal changes. AI developers must continuously monitor and improve their models to align with ethical standards and emerging best practices.

9. Mitigating Harmful Applications:

- Responsible Deployment: Considerations must be made to avoid deploying NLP models in applications that can cause harm or violate ethical principles, such as automated harassment, discrimination, or misinformation generation.

Addressing ethical considerations in data usage is crucial for the responsible development of NLP models and AI systems. By focusing on fairness, privacy, transparency, and accountability, developers can ensure that their NLP applications benefit society while minimizing harm and bias. Ethical guidelines and responsible AI practices are integral to building trust and confidence in AI technologies.

Chapter 7: Evaluation and Metrics

In this chapter, we explore the critical aspects of evaluating Natural Language Processing (NLP) models and understanding their performance. This includes common evaluation metrics, techniques like cross-validation, and the importance of model interpretability.

7.1. Common NLP Evaluation Metrics

Evaluating Natural Language Processing (NLP) models accurately is essential for understanding their performance. Here are common NLP evaluation metrics and their significance, along with code examples:

1. Accuracy:

- Definition: Accuracy measures the proportion of correctly predicted instances out of the total. It's a simple and intuitive metric for classification tasks.

- Code Example:

```
from sklearn.metrics import accuracy_score

true_labels = [0, 1, 0, 1, 1]
predicted_labels = [0, 1, 0, 1, 0]

accuracy = accuracy_score(true_labels, predicted_labels)
print(f'Accuracy: {accuracy:.2f}')
```

2. Precision and Recall:

- Precision: Precision measures the accuracy of positive predictions. It answers, "Of all the predicted positives, how many were correct?"

- Recall: Recall measures the model's ability to capture all positive instances. It answers, "Of all the actual positives, how many did the model correctly predict?"

- Code Example:

```python
from sklearn.metrics import precision_score,
recall_score

true_labels = [0, 1, 0, 1, 1]
predicted_labels = [0, 1, 0, 1, 0]

precision           =           precision_score(true_labels,
predicted_labels)
recall = recall_score(true_labels, predicted_labels)

print(f'Precision: {precision:.2f}')
print(f'Recall: {recall:.2f}')
```

3. F1-Score:

- Definition: The F1-score is the harmonic mean of precision and recall. It provides a balanced measure of a model's performance, especially when dealing with imbalanced datasets.

- **Code Example:**

```python
from sklearn.metrics import f1_score

true_labels = [0, 1, 0, 1, 1]
predicted_labels = [0, 1, 0, 1, 0]

f1 = f1_score(true_labels, predicted_labels)
print(f'F1-Score: {f1:.2f}')
```

4. BLEU Score:

- Definition: The BLEU (Bilingual Evaluation Understudy) score is commonly used for machine translation tasks. It compares model-generated translations to reference translations based on n-grams (contiguous sequences of words).

- **Code Example (Using the NLTK library):**

```python
from nltk.translate.bleu_score import sentence_bleu

reference = [['this', 'is', 'a', 'test']]
candidate = ['this', 'is', 'a', 'test']
```

```
score = sentence_bleu(reference, candidate)
print(f'BLEU Score: {score:.2f}')
```

5. ROUGE Score:

- Definition: The ROUGE (Recall-Oriented Understudy for Gisting Evaluation) score measures the overlap between model-generated text and reference text. It's often used for text summarization tasks.

- Code Example (Using the NLTK library):

```
from nltk.translate.bleu_score import corpus_bleu

references = [['this', 'is', 'a', 'test']]
candidates = [['this', 'is', 'a', 'test']]

score = corpus_bleu(references, candidates)
print(f'ROUGE Score: {score:.2f}')
```

6. Perplexity:

- Definition: Perplexity assesses the language model's performance by quantifying how well it predicts text. Lower perplexity indicates better model performance.

- Code Example (Using a language model):

```
from nltk.lm import MLE
from nltk.util import bigrams

text = [['this', 'is', 'a', 'test'], ['another', 'example', 'sentence']]
model = MLE(2)
model.fit(bigrams(text), text)

perplexity = model.perplexity(['this', 'is', 'a', 'test'])
print(f'Perplexity: {perplexity:.2f}')
```

These common NLP evaluation metrics provide insights into different aspects of model performance, such as accuracy, precision, recall, and language generation quality. Choosing the appropriate metric depends on the specific NLP task and the goals of your model.

7.2. Cross-Validation and Test Set

Cross-validation and test sets are crucial techniques for assessing the performance and generalization of Natural Language Processing (NLP) models. Here's a detailed explanation of these concepts, along with code examples:

1. Cross-Validation:

- Definition: Cross-validation is a resampling procedure used to evaluate machine learning models on a limited data sample. It provides insights into how well a model will generalize to unseen data.

- K-Fold Cross-Validation: One common method is k-fold cross-validation. It involves dividing the dataset into k subsets (folds), training the model on k-1 folds, and testing it on the remaining fold. This process is repeated k times, with each fold serving as the test set once.

- Stratified Cross-Validation: In NLP, where class imbalances are common, stratified cross-validation ensures that each fold maintains the same class distribution as the original dataset.

- Code Example (Using scikit-learn):

```
from sklearn.model_selection import cross_val_score,
StratifiedKFold
from sklearn.linear_model import LogisticRegression

# Load your dataset
X, y = load_nlp_data()

# Initialize a model
model = LogisticRegression()

# Create a StratifiedKFold object for cross-validation
cv = StratifiedKFold(n_splits=5, shuffle=True,
random_state=42)

# Perform cross-validation and get accuracy scores
scores = cross_val_score(model, X, y, cv=cv)

print("Cross-Validation Scores:")
```

```
for i, score in enumerate(scores):
    print(f"Fold {i + 1}: {score:.2f}")
```

2. Test Set:

- Definition: The test set is a separate dataset that is not used during model training or hyperparameter tuning. It is reserved for the final evaluation of a trained model's performance.

- Purpose: The test set provides an unbiased estimate of how well the model will perform on new, unseen data. It helps assess the model's generalization capabilities.

- Code Example (Using scikit-learn):

```
from sklearn.model_selection import train_test_split
from sklearn.metrics import accuracy_score
from sklearn.linear_model import LogisticRegression

# Load your dataset
X, y = load_nlp_data()
```

```python
# Split the dataset into training and test sets
X_train, X_test, y_train, y_test =
train_test_split(X, y, test_size=0.2,
random_state=42)

# Initialize and train a model
model = LogisticRegression()
model.fit(X_train, y_train)

# Make predictions on the test set
y_pred = model.predict(X_test)

# Evaluate the model using accuracy
accuracy = accuracy_score(y_test, y_pred)
print(f"Test Set Accuracy: {accuracy:.2f}")
```

Cross-validation helps assess a model's performance under different conditions, reducing the risk of overfitting. The test set, on the other hand, provides a final evaluation of the model's performance on completely unseen data, ensuring that the model generalizes well to real-world scenarios. Both techniques are essential for building and validating robust NLP models.

7.3. Model Interpretability

Model interpretability is a critical aspect of Natural Language Processing (NLP) and machine learning, as it enables us to understand how models make predictions. Here's a comprehensive exploration of model interpretability in NLP with explanations and code examples:

1. Why Model Interpretability Matters:

- Trust and Transparency: Interpretability helps build trust in machine learning models by providing insights into their decision-making processes. It makes models more transparent and understandable to both technical and non-technical stakeholders.

- Debugging: Interpretability aids in identifying and addressing issues in models. When a model makes unexpected predictions, understanding the reasons behind those predictions is crucial for debugging.

- Ethical Considerations: In NLP, it's essential to ensure that models do not produce biased or harmful outputs. Interpretability tools can help detect and mitigate biases.

2. Techniques for Model Interpretability:

- Attention Maps: Attention mechanisms in models like Transformers can produce attention scores, indicating which parts of the input data the model focuses on. These scores can be visualized to understand what the model finds important.

- Feature Importance: For traditional machine learning models, feature importance methods like permutation importance, SHAP values, or feature contribution plots reveal the impact of input features on predictions.

- LIME (Local Interpretable Model-agnostic Explanations): LIME is a technique that approximates the model's behavior locally by perturbing the input data and observing how predictions change. It provides interpretable explanations for individual predictions.

- Interpretable Models: Some models, like decision trees or linear regression, are inherently interpretable. Using these models in NLP tasks can simplify interpretability.

- Explainable AI (XAI) Libraries: Several libraries, such as the InterpretML library for Microsoft's AutoML, provide tools and interfaces for model interpretability.

3. Visualizing Attention Maps (Using Transformers):

```
import transformers
import torch
import matplotlib.pyplot as plt

# Load a pre-trained transformer model
model_name = 'bert-base-uncased'
tokenizer =
transformers.AutoTokenizer.from_pretrained(model
_name)
```

```python
model =
transformers.AutoModel.from_pretrained(model_na
me)

# Tokenize and encode input text
text = "This is an example sentence."
tokens = tokenizer(text, return_tensors='pt')
outputs = model(tokens)

# Extract attention weights from the model
attention_weights = outputs['attentions']

# Visualize attention for a specific layer and head
layer = 5
head = 2
attention =
attention_weights[layer][0][head].detach().numpy()

# Plot attention scores as a heatmap
plt.imshow(attention, cmap='viridis', aspect='auto')
plt.title(f'Layer {layer}, Head {head}')
plt.colorbar()
plt.xlabel('Input Tokens')
```

```python
plt.ylabel('Attention Weights')
plt.show()
```

4. Using SHAP Values for Feature Importance (Using scikit-learn and SHAP):

```python
import shap
from sklearn.ensemble import
RandomForestClassifier

# Load your NLP dataset
X, y = load_nlp_data()

# Initialize a model
model = RandomForestClassifier()

# Fit the model
model.fit(X, y)

# Initialize an explainer
explainer = shap.Explainer(model, X)

# Explain a single prediction
```

```
sample_idx = 0
shap_values = explainer.shap_values(X[sample_idx])

# Visualize feature importance using summary_plot
shap.summary_plot(shap_values, X[sample_idx],
feature_names=feature_names)
```

Model interpretability techniques are essential for making NLP models more transparent, accountable, and trustworthy. These techniques help ensure that models provide accurate, unbiased, and ethically sound predictions, making them suitable for real-world applications.

Chapter 8: Deploying Transformer Models

This chapter covers the crucial steps and considerations for deploying Transformer models in production NLP applications. It includes model serialization, integration with web applications, scaling for production, and ongoing monitoring and maintenance.

8.1. Model Serialization and Saving

When deploying Transformer models for production use in Natural Language Processing (NLP) applications, it's essential to serialize and save your trained models efficiently. Here's an in-depth look at model serialization and saving, along with code examples:

1. Model Serialization:

- Definition: Model serialization refers to the process of converting a trained model, including its architecture and learned parameters, into a format that can be efficiently stored and loaded when needed for inference.

- Purpose: Serialization is crucial for model deployment because it allows you to save and share your model with others and deploy it to production servers without having to retrain it each time.

2. Saving Models in PyTorch:

In PyTorch, you can save and load models using the `torch.save()` and `torch.load()` functions. Here's a step-by-step example:

Saving a Model:

```
import torch

# Define and train your Transformer model
model = ...
```

```python
# Save the trained model to a file
torch.save(model.state_dict(),
"transformer_model.pt")
```

Loading a Model:

```python
# Load the saved model
model = YourTransformerModel()  # Instantiate your
model class
model.load_state_dict(torch.load("transformer_mode
l.pt"))
model.eval()  # Set the model to evaluation mode
```

3. Saving Models in TensorFlow:

In TensorFlow, you can use the SavedModel format for serialization. Here's how to save and load models:

Saving a Model:

```python
import tensorflow as tf
```

```python
# Define and train your Transformer model
```

```
model = ...
```

```
# Save the trained model in the SavedModel format
model.save("transformer_model")
```

Loading a Model:

```
# Load the saved model
loaded_model =
tf.keras.models.load_model("transformer_model")
```

4. Model Serialization in Scikit-Learn:

For Scikit-Learn models, you can use the `joblib` library for serialization. Here's an example:

Saving a Scikit-Learn Model:

```
import joblib
```

```
# Define and train your Scikit-Learn model
model = ...
```

```
# Save the trained model
joblib.dump(model, "scikit_learn_model.pkl")
```

Loading a Scikit-Learn Model:

```
# Load the saved Scikit-Learn model
loaded_model = joblib.load("scikit_learn_model.pkl")
```

Serialization allows you to save your trained Transformer model in a file, making it portable and ready for deployment. You can then load the model in your production environment, allowing it to make predictions on new data without having to retrain it. This is a crucial step in the model deployment pipeline.

8.2. Integration with Web Applications

Integrating Transformer models into web applications is a common requirement for deploying Natural Language Processing (NLP) solutions. This section provides a detailed explanation of the key considerations and steps involved in this integration, along with code examples.

1. Choosing a Web Framework:

- Web Framework Selection: Begin by selecting a web framework suitable for your web application. Popular options include Flask, Django, and FastAPI. Your choice depends on factors like project complexity and your familiarity with the framework.

2. Creating API Endpoints:

- Defining API Endpoints: API endpoints are URLs within your web application that handle specific tasks. You should define endpoints for model inference and any other functionalities your NLP application requires.

3. Handling HTTP Requests:

- Parsing Input Data: Use the web framework's request handling capabilities to parse incoming data from HTTP requests. This data typically includes text inputs that need to be processed by your Transformer model.

4. Model Integration:

- Loading the Transformer Model: Before you can make predictions, load your pre-trained Transformer model into memory. Ensure the model is in evaluation mode (`model.eval()` in PyTorch) to disable dropout and ensure consistent inference.

- Model Inference: Use the loaded model to make predictions on the input data obtained from the HTTP requests. Ensure you preprocess the data (e.g., tokenization) to match the format expected by the model.

5. Handling Responses:

- Formatting Results: Once you have model predictions, format them as JSON or another suitable format for the HTTP response. This makes it easier for clients to consume the results.

6. Example Using Flask:

Below is a simplified example of integrating a Transformer model into a Flask web application. This example assumes you've already trained a Transformer model and saved it.

```python
from flask import Flask, request, jsonify
import torch

app = Flask(__name__)

# Load your pre-trained Transformer model
model = torch.load("transformer_model.pt")
model.eval()

@app.route("/predict", methods=["POST"])
def predict():
    try:
        # Parse input data from the HTTP request
        data = request.json
        text = data["text"]

        # Preprocess input (e.g., tokenization)
```

```python
        # Make predictions with the loaded model
        prediction = model(text)

        # Format the response
        response = {"prediction": prediction}

        return jsonify(response)

    except Exception as e:
        return jsonify({"error": str(e)}), 400

if __name__ == "__main__":
    app.run(debug=True)
```

This Flask application defines a `/predict` endpoint that accepts JSON input with a "text" field. It loads a pre-trained model, makes predictions, and returns the results as JSON.

Integrating a Transformer model into a web application enables users to interact with your NLP solution through a user-friendly interface. Carefully consider your web framework, data handling, and response formatting to create a robust and efficient integration.

8.3. Scaling Models for Production

Scaling Transformer models for production in Natural Language Processing (NLP) applications is essential to ensure that your models can handle large volumes of requests efficiently. This section provides an in-depth explanation of the key considerations and strategies for scaling models, along with code examples.

1. Containerization and Orchestration:

- Containerization: Containerization technologies like Docker provide a way to package your application and its dependencies into a portable container. Containers can run consistently across various environments, making them ideal for scaling.

- Orchestration: Orchestration tools like Kubernetes can manage and scale containers in a cluster. Kubernetes automates tasks such as load balancing, scaling, and service discovery, ensuring high availability.

2. Scaling Strategies:

- Horizontal Scaling: In a production environment, you can scale your model horizontally by deploying multiple instances of your containerized application. Load balancers distribute incoming requests across these instances.

- Vertical Scaling: Alternatively, you can vertically scale your model by using more powerful hardware or increasing the resources allocated to each container instance. This approach may be necessary for very resource-intensive models.

3. Serverless Computing:

- Serverless Platforms: Serverless computing platforms like AWS Lambda and Azure Functions allow you to deploy code as functions that automatically scale in response to incoming requests. This can be a cost-effective way to handle variable workloads.

- Function as a Service (FaaS): By deploying your model as a serverless function, you offload infrastructure management to the platform, allowing you to focus on writing code.

4. Load Balancing:

- Load Balancers: Implement load balancing to evenly distribute incoming requests across multiple instances of your application. This ensures high availability and efficient resource utilization.

5. Auto Scaling:

- Auto Scaling Policies: Use auto scaling policies to automatically adjust the number of container instances based on metrics like CPU utilization or request rate. This ensures that your application can handle varying workloads.

6. Caching:

- Result Caching: Implement result caching to store and retrieve frequently requested results. Caching can significantly reduce the computational load on your model for repeated requests with the same input data.

7. Example with Kubernetes:

Here's a simplified example of deploying a containerized Flask application (with a Transformer model) on Kubernetes:

```yaml
# kubernetes_deployment.yaml

apiVersion: apps/v1
kind: Deployment
metadata:
  name: nlp-app
spec:
  replicas: 3  # Number of desired replicas
  selector:
    matchLabels:
```

```yaml
    app: nlp-app
  template:
    metadata:
      labels:
        app: nlp-app
    spec:
      containers:
        - name: nlp-container
          image: your-nlp-app-image:latest
          ports:
            - containerPort: 80
---
apiVersion: v1
kind: Service
metadata:
  name: nlp-service
spec:
  selector:
    app: nlp-app
  ports:
    - protocol: TCP
      port: 80
      targetPort: 80
```

```
type: LoadBalancer
```

This Kubernetes deployment creates three replicas of your containerized NLP application and exposes them through a LoadBalancer service, distributing incoming traffic.

Scaling Transformer models for production is crucial to ensure that your NLP applications can handle high loads efficiently and provide a responsive user experience. By utilizing containerization, orchestration, auto scaling, and caching, you can build a scalable and reliable production environment for your models.

Chapter 9: Future Trends and Challenges

This chapter explores the evolving landscape of Transformer models in Natural Language Processing (NLP) and the associated trends, challenges, and ethical considerations.

9.1. Recent Advances in Transformers

Recent years have witnessed significant advancements in Transformer models, revolutionizing the field of Natural Language Processing (NLP). Here's an in-depth exploration of these breakthroughs:

1. Multimodal Transformers:

- Definition: Multimodal Transformers combine text and image processing capabilities within a single model. They can understand and generate text descriptions for images, making them highly versatile.

- Examples: Notable models include CLIP (Contrastive Language-Image Pretraining) and ALIGN (Attentional LInguistic Image Network), which have demonstrated the ability to link images and text effectively.

- Applications: Multimodal Transformers find applications in image captioning, visual question answering, and more. They enable NLP models to understand and generate text based on visual information.

2. Large-Scale Models:

- Definition: Large-scale models are Transformer architectures with billions or even trillions of parameters. Examples include GPT-3, GPT-4, and models like Switch Transformers.

- Performance: These models achieve state-of-the-art performance on a wide range of NLP tasks. They exhibit remarkable language understanding and generation capabilities.

- Challenges: Training, fine-tuning, and deploying such massive models present computational challenges, and their environmental impact due to energy consumption is a concern.

3. Few-Shot Learning:

- Definition: Few-shot learning refers to the ability of models to generalize and make accurate predictions with very few examples. Models like GPT-3 have demonstrated extraordinary few-shot capabilities.

- Flexibility: Few-shot learning opens up possibilities for more adaptable NLP systems. These models can answer questions, translate languages, or perform other tasks with minimal examples.

- Use Cases: Few-shot learning is valuable in scenarios where collecting extensive labeled data is challenging or time-consuming.

4. Low-Resource Languages:

- Definition: Low-resource languages are languages with limited data and resources available for NLP. Recent advances aim to extend NLP capabilities to these languages.

- Challenges: Low-resource languages often lack large datasets and pretrained models, making it challenging to build effective NLP systems.

- Efforts: Researchers are working on techniques like cross-lingual transfer learning and data augmentation to bridge the gap between resource-rich and resource-poor languages.

These recent advances in Transformers have expanded the possibilities and capabilities of NLP models. They empower models to work with multimodal data, handle low-resource languages, generalize from minimal examples, and perform at unprecedented scales. However, they also bring challenges related to computational resources, ethical considerations, and environmental impact that require ongoing research and attention.

9.2. Open Challenges in NLP

Despite the remarkable progress in Natural Language Processing (NLP), several open challenges persist in the field. These challenges have significant implications for the responsible development and deployment of NLP models. Let's get into these challenges in detail:

1. Bias and Fairness:

- Challenge: NLP models can inherit biases present in their training data, leading to unfair or discriminatory predictions. Addressing bias and ensuring fairness in NLP models is a paramount challenge.

- Implications: Biased models can perpetuate social inequalities and lead to biased decisions in applications like hiring, lending, and content recommendation.

2. Explainability and Interpretability:

- Challenge: As NLP models grow in complexity, understanding their decisions becomes challenging. Ensuring that users can interpret and trust model outputs is essential.

- Implications: Lack of explainability can hinder model adoption in critical applications like healthcare and finance, where decision-making transparency is crucial.

3. Data Privacy:

- Challenge: NLP models often deal with sensitive data, such as medical records or personal messages. Protecting user data during training and deployment is a top concern.

- Implications: Data breaches or privacy violations can have severe legal and ethical consequences, eroding user trust in NLP applications.

4. Multilingual NLP:

- Challenge: Extending NLP capabilities to low-resource languages and dialects remains a significant challenge. Many languages lack the data and resources needed to build effective models.

- Implications: Neglecting low-resource languages limits access to NLP technologies and reinforces language divides.

5. Few-Shot and Zero-Shot Learning:

- Challenge: While few-shot and zero-shot learning have advanced, improving model performance with extremely limited training examples remains challenging.

- Implications: Robust few-shot learning could empower users to adapt models to specific tasks without requiring extensive labeled data.

6. Fine-Grained Understanding:

- Challenge: NLP models often lack fine-grained understanding of context, humor, sarcasm, or cultural nuances, limiting their ability to engage in nuanced conversations.

- Implications: Incomplete understanding can lead to miscommunications and misinterpretations, especially in chatbots and customer support applications.

7. Adversarial Attacks:

- Challenge: NLP models are susceptible to adversarial attacks, where intentionally crafted inputs can mislead the model's predictions.

- Implications: Adversarial attacks can be exploited for misinformation campaigns, spam, and other malicious purposes.

8. Resource Efficiency:

- Challenge: Training and deploying large-scale models consume substantial computational resources and energy. Finding ways to make NLP more resource-efficient is a pressing concern.

- Implications: High resource consumption contributes to environmental concerns and limits accessibility to small organizations and researchers.

9.3. Ethical and Societal Implications

As Natural Language Processing (NLP) technologies continue to advance, it's essential to recognize and address their ethical and societal implications. This section explores the broader consequences of NLP's development and deployment:

1. Misinformation and Disinformation:

- Challenge: NLP models can generate highly convincing fake text, which can be used to spread misinformation and disinformation at scale.

- Implications: This can impact public opinion, elections, and even public health, as seen during the COVID-19 pandemic.

2. Surveillance and Privacy:

- Challenge: NLP is used in surveillance applications, including text analysis of social media and email content.

- Implications: This raises concerns about privacy violations and the potential for surveillance states, where citizens' communications are constantly monitored.

3. Job Disruption:

- Challenge: NLP models are increasingly capable of automating tasks like content generation, translation, and customer service.

- Implications: While automation can lead to efficiency, it can also disrupt industries and lead to job displacement, requiring workforce adaptation and upskilling.

4. Environmental Impact:

- Challenge: Training large-scale NLP models requires significant computational resources and energy.

- Implications: This contributes to environmental concerns, as energy consumption associated with deep learning models can have a notable carbon footprint.

5. Bias and Discrimination:

- Challenge: NLP models can perpetuate biases present in training data, leading to biased or discriminatory outcomes.

- Implications: Bias in NLP can affect marginalized communities and reinforce existing social inequalities.

6. Content Moderation:

- Challenge: NLP is used in content moderation on social media platforms to detect and remove harmful or inappropriate content.

- Implications: Striking the right balance between freedom of speech and preventing harm remains a complex and ethically charged challenge.

7. Ethical AI:

- Challenge: Ensuring that AI and NLP technologies are developed and deployed ethically requires clear guidelines and standards.

- Implications: Ethical AI principles should guide decisions about model behavior, data usage, and transparency to prevent harm and protect users' rights.

8. Accessibility and Inclusion:

- Challenge: Ensuring that NLP technologies are accessible to all, including those with disabilities or in low-resource regions, is an ongoing challenge.

- Implications: Lack of accessibility can exacerbate inequalities and limit the benefits of NLP to certain groups.

9. Accountability and Regulation:

- Challenge: The rapid advancement of NLP often outpaces regulation and oversight.

- Implications: Establishing clear regulations and accountability frameworks is essential to prevent misuse and ensure responsible development and deployment.

Addressing these ethical and societal implications requires a multi-stakeholder approach involving researchers, industry leaders, policymakers, and civil society. It involves developing ethical guidelines, considering the impact on vulnerable populations, and continuously monitoring and adapting NLP technologies to align with societal values and priorities. Responsible development and use of NLP can unlock its transformative potential while minimizing harm.

Conclusion

The field of Natural Language Processing (NLP) has undergone a profound transformation, largely driven by the advent of Transformer models. These models, with their self-attention mechanisms and deep architecture, have revolutionized the way we process, understand, and generate human language. In this comprehensive guide, we have explored the various facets of NLP, focusing on the Transformer architecture and its practical applications. Here's a summary of what we've covered:

Understanding Natural Language Processing (NLP):

NLP is the bridge between human language and machines, enabling them to comprehend, interpret, and generate text. It has wide-ranging applications, from chatbots and language translation to sentiment analysis and more.

The Rise of Transformers:

The emergence of Transformers, introduced in the 2017 paper "Attention is All You Need," marked a pivotal moment in NLP. Their self-attention mechanism has made them the backbone of state-of-the-art NLP models due to their ability to understand context effectively.

Goals and Scope of This Book:

Our primary goal was to provide a practical understanding of the Transformer architecture and its application in NLP. We've journeyed from fundamentals to hands-on implementation, equipping you to build and fine-tune your own Transformer models for various NLP tasks.

Prerequisites and Assumptions:

To make the most of this book, it's helpful to have some programming experience, familiarity with Python, and a basic understanding of machine learning concepts. We've assumed that you're eager to explore the world of NLP and Transformer models.

Fundamentals of Transformers:

We explored the birth of Transformers, explained the key components, and provided an overview of their architecture. Understanding these fundamentals is essential for building and fine-tuning Transformer models.

Preprocessing and Data Preparation:

We discussed data collection, cleaning, tokenization, vocabulary creation, data encoding, padding, data augmentation, and dataset splitting, setting the stage for model training.

Building Transformer Models:

You learned about model architecture choices, implementing Transformers from scratch, utilizing pretrained models, and fine-tuning and customizing models for your specific NLP tasks.

Training and Optimization:

We covered loss functions, gradient descent, optimizers, learning rate scheduling, overfitting, and training best practices to help you achieve optimal model performance.

Applications of Transformers in NLP:

Explore the practical use cases of Transformers in chatbots, sentiment analysis, machine translation, and question answering, understanding how these models can transform real-world problems.

Handling Real-World Data:

Discover how to deal with challenges such as imbalanced data, noisy text, and ethical considerations when using data in NLP applications.

Evaluation and Metrics:

Understand common NLP evaluation metrics, cross-validation, test sets, and model interpretability, crucial for assessing and improving model performance.

Deploying Transformer Models:

Learn how to serialize and save models, integrate them with web applications, scale them for production, and ensure monitoring and maintenance for robust deployment.

Future Trends and Challenges:

We examined recent advances in Transformers, open challenges in NLP, and ethical and societal implications. Staying informed about these trends and challenges is essential for responsible NLP development.

In conclusion, the world of NLP is continually evolving, with Transformers at the forefront of innovation. As you embark on your NLP journey, keep in mind the ethical considerations, challenges, and potential impacts of your work. Responsible development and deployment of NLP technologies can lead to transformative applications that benefit society while mitigating risks and challenges.

www.ingramcontent.com/pod-product-compliance
Lightning Source LLC
LaVergne TN
LVHW051338050326
832903LV00031B/3612